HANA
A Photographic History of Hawaii's Paradise

By Bruce McAllister

Copyright © 2017 Bruce McAllister

All rights reserved. No part of this book may be reproduced, stored in a retrieval system, or transmitted in any form or by any means without written permission of the publisher. Photographs with no credit line are from the author's collection or public domain.

Roundup Press

Boulder, CO 80301

www.wingsalcan.com

ISBN: 978-0-692-86620-7

ISBN 10: 0-692-86620-5

Distributed by Bess Press, Honolulu, HI www.besspress.com

Printed by: C & C Offset Printing, China

Front Cover: Morris Pi'ilani throw-net fishing near Hamoa. © Bruce McAllister
Back Cover: Alau Island is a bird sanctuary off the east coast of Hana, near Hamoa. Two palm trees stand out on the summit. Some people think that the trees were planted to commemorate a father's loss of his sons in World War II. Every year, there is an outrigger canoe race from Hana Bay to Alau Island and back. Alau Island is named after Prince Alau, who was one of the many Maui monarchs who preceded Pi'ilani the Great.

Contents

Acknowledgments	vi
Introduction	9
Old Hana	25
The 1946 Tsunami	37
The Hana Highway	45
Pi'ilanihale Heiau	60
Paul Fagan: Cattle, Hotel & Baseball	67
Hotel Hana-Maui	89
Faces of Hana	107
Hasegawa General Store	127
Eddie Pu	135
Beaches	145
Hana by Air	161
Kipahulu and Lindbergh	175
Kaupo	197
Haleakala	211
Hana's Celebrities	225
Bibliography	230
About the Author	232

Acknowledgments

Amy Mendolia / Gilbert & Associates

Alix Prejean

Ashley Cothran / Travaasa Experiential Resorts

Dot Pua, Hana's Hairdresser

Hana Cultural Center

Harolen Kaiwi

Hawaii Historical Society

Matson Lines

Maui Historical Society

National Park Service

NOAA

Neil Hasegawa

San Francisco Public Library

Thomas Hill, Lampas Books, Design

Tia Reber / Bishop Museum

Vance & Marlene Pu

Dedicated to the people of Hana

Downtown Hana in the 1920s. The sugar mill dominated the landscape.
Hawaii State Archives

Introduction

My first trip to Hana was in the late 1940s. At the time it was a sleepy, isolated Hawaiian town without many *haoles* (mainlanders, whites, and tourists). As a pre-teenager, I was about to learn how to body surf and live without electricity in Puuiki where my parents had just bought a modest house with a great view of the Pacific Ocean.

Paul Fagan, a San Francisco industrialist, had talked my parents into buying a second home in Hana. And he was about to do something much more radical. Like turn Hana's sugar cane fields into a town-saving luxury hotel! At the end of World War II, there was no Hawaiian hotel outside Waikiki. He could hardly have chosen a more obscure location.

It had been only twenty years since Hana, on the island of Maui, connected to the outside world by a rough dirt road, and it would be almost two decades more before it was paved and turned into the infamous Hana Highway, a narrow road with over fifty one-lane bridges and countless torturous curves.

To get publicity for his hotel venture, he enlisted the help of the San Francisco Seals baseball team, which he also owned. He brought the team to Hana for spring training and invited along a boatload of sportswriters who would turn out glowing reviews of "heavenly Hana" for readers back on the mainland.

I too loved Hana from the first day I set foot there. As a young aspiring photographer, I took photos of locals, beaches, and anything that moved. The local commercial photographer, a Filipino, took me under his wing and taught me how to develop film and make prints in his studio on Main Street.

This book covers life and sights in the Hana area, from its sugar cane days right up to the present. I never lived full-time in Hana, but I did learn to body surf there, pass my first driver's license test, mix with the locals, drag race at the Hana airport at night, swim at Hamoa Beach in moonlight, and enjoy movies once a week at the movie theater (which is now the Hasegawa General Store).

Christian Hedemann was a Danish mechanical engineer who settled in Hawaii in 1878, where he worked at the Hana Sugar Plantation and the Honolulu Iron Works. He is, however, remembered primarily as an avid amateur photographer who helped found the Hawaiian Camera Club (1889–1893). His photographs of native peoples, landscapes, families, and industry offer a unique pictorial record of Hawaii at the end of the 19th century. Hedemann took this self-portrait in Hana in March 1884.
© C. J. Hedemann / Bishop Museum

Photographer Christian J. Hedemann took this Hana family portrait circa 1883. The husband probably was J. K. Iosepa who became the minister of Wananalua Church the same year.
© C. J. Hedemann / Bishop Museum

Hawaii State Archives

Kaupo grass house, circa 1915. Hawaii Historical Society Photograph Collection

Grass house on Maui, circa 1908. Hawaiian Historical Society Photograph Collection

(Left) Life in Kaupo in the 1800s was simple. Lava rock and thatched roofing weatherproofed homes, and outrigger canoes were the preferred means of getting around the islands. Kaupo was "Wahipana" (Special Place) for ancient Hawaiians. In the early 1900s many families lived in Kaupo. Fishing, farming, hunting and ranching were primary occupations. In 1859 the district was combined with that of Hana. Hawaii State Archives

In the early 1900s, a Hana Bay view from the bluff.
Hawaii State Archives

Over 500 years ago, the island of Maui was opened up for trade by the King's Trail. It was originally built by native Hawaiians under the reign of Maui chiefs Pi'ilani and Kihapi'ilani, but was revitalized in the 1800s by prisoners. It was four to six feet wide, 138 miles long, and paved with hand-fitted lava rocks. In recent times, the trail became a historical landmark. Library of Congress

Hana Harbor and Ka'uiki Hill, Hana, 1900.
© Maui Historical Society

The Matson *SS Enterprise* loading sugarcane at Hana Harbor, 1926. © Maui Historical Society

Loading facility at Kipahulu when ships were the only way to move goods on Maui. Hawaii State Archives

1920 Hana Scout Troop. Maui Historical Society

(Above) A Japanese submarine. After Pearl Harbor, Japanese submarines sunk only three ships in Hawaiian waters during the rest of the war. Unfortunately, the *Royal T. Frank* (next page) was one of those.

As a child growing up in Hana, Ramona Ho heard her father, Joseph Cabral, tell stories about the day he and his classmates helped rescue thirty-three survivors from the *Royal T. Frank*, a U.S. Army transport ship sunk by a Japanese torpedo off Maui's Hana Coast in January 1942.

The *Royal T. Frank*'s final voyage occurred in a particularly tense time period in Hawaii. Japanese submarines were active in Hawaiian waters and had already sunk three ships. A submarine had also surfaced to shell Maui's Kahului Harbor, and others had fired at Hilo on the Big Island and Nawiliwili Harbor on Kauai. As a precaution, on its final voyage, the *Royal T. Frank* was part of a three-ship convoy that included a Navy destroyer and a tug. Aboard were 26 U.S. Army Japanese-American recruits from the Big Island who had just completed boot camp at Schofield Barracks on O'ahu.

Less than two months after the attack on Pearl Harbor on the evening of January 28, 1942, while steaming from Kahului, Maui to Hilo, the *Royal T. Frank* was towing an ammunition barge loaded with petroleum and building materials. About two miles off the coast of Hana, Maui the General Frank was torpedoed by the Japanese Kaidai VIa late class

KD6 submarine I-171. The Frank exploded and sank in less than thirty seconds in the 6,000 feet deep Alenuihaha Channel between Maui and the Big Island. Covered in oil, the survivors spent hours in the ocean, many clinging to whatever debris they could, before the ammunition barge that had been the actual target of the Japanese submarine picked them up.

"My father had told us the story since we were very little," says Ms. Ho. "The survivors had come ashore while Dad was at school . . . [Most were] covered with oil and were naked." Drilled for just such an incident by their principal, William P. Haia, the students hurried the men to the school, helped them clean up, and assembled cots for them. The Navy flew in a medic to treat them until an ambulance could traverse the winding Hana road to bring the men out. A day later, the survivors were gone—and soon, so was the story. On February 1, 1944, off the island of Bougainville in New Guinea, American depth charges sunk the same Japanese submarine that had sunk the *Royal T. Frank* two years earlier.

Main Street Hana in the early 1930s.
© Hasegawa / Bishop Museum

Old Hana

In Hana, horses were as common as cars in the old days. Electricity was restricted to the town itself. People used kerosene lanterns. Entertainment? There was a movie theater in Hana that had one movie a week. And that was only if the town's worn-out diesel generators did not break down. And there never have been any traffic lights. The original Hotel Hana-Maui had a big show and buffet every Sunday night.

Hana's first plantation was owned and operated by George Wilfong. He imported Chinese laborers to Hana in 1852 after the local Hawaiians balked at his questionable labor contracts. He offered low-ball, ten-year contracts to his Chinese workers for one hundred and fifty dollars cash. Eventually his plantation operation failed, as more competitors moved in.

Almost a century later, Hana's population declined from a high of 3,500 to seven hundred permanent inhabitants—a world apart from the rest of Maui (In 2010, Hana's population was 1,235). Sugar cane was the only thing that kept the area going. Starting in 1946, Paul Fagan revitalized Hana, starting the Hotel Hana-Maui and bringing in cattle from Molokai. This stabilized the community and helped employment. The infamous Hana Highway has always protected Hana from high-rise hotels and golf courses. With a small population, it has always had the feel of an old Hawaiian community, set in a heavenly landscape of banyan, mango, and breadfruit trees. Hana only received television in 1977 and still has no stoplights.

A hukilau at Koki Beach in 1936.
© Harold T. Stearns / Bishop Museum

The first bookmobile in Hawaii hit the road on Maui in 1926—a Ford roadster, complete with rumble seat. The bookmobile got upgraded in 1932 with a half-ton Ford delivery van with shelves and side panels that lifted up to make book-filled counters. By 1938, there was a fleet of bookmobiles delivering books throughout the state. Hawaii State Archives

Early Ke'anae had more taro patches than houses.

Kalani Castro succumbed to tuberculosis, just like many other Hawaiians. Since the 1800s, many native Hawaiians contracted diseases from people immigrating to Hawaii from the Far East and other countries. In the year 2000, it was estimated that there were fewer than seven thousand full-blooded Hawaiians still in Hawaii.
© Bruce McAllister

(Left) Wananalua Congregational Church is a historic 19th-century building and listed with the National Register of Historic Places. Hawaii State Archives

Officer William F. Roback served his community from Ke'anae to Kaupo in the Hana District for more than thirty years. On April 13, 1958, he was killed while escorting a prisoner to Wailuku.
Courtesy Maui County Police Dept.

Peter Pi'ilani at Hamoa Beach circa 1949. © Bruce McAllister

One of the Koko brothers in the early 1950s. He had fifteen brothers and sisters. © Bruce McAllister

© Bruce McAllister

The 1946 Tsunami hit Hilo without much warning. Newly installed sensors in the Aleutian Islands failed to provide any advance warning. National Oceanographic and Atmospheric Administration

2 The 1946 Tsunami

The April 1, 1946, tsunami devastated Hawaii. Originating in the Aleutian Island Chain, it first wiped out Hilo. Over a fifteen-minute period, the wave struck about seven times, killing 159 people. Most of the deaths were in Hilo and Laupahoehoe on the Big Island of Hawaii. The maximum height of the tidal wave was fifty-five feet in the Pololu Valley, thirty-six feet on Oahu, and thirty-three feet on Maui.

But Hana was also hit hard. "Then I seen my aunty up there. They brought her up. She was on a truck and she didn't have no clothes . . . the waves—this wave take everybody's clothes . . . so my mom dress her up and then they take her to the Hana Hospital. But on the way she die." —Harry Pahukoa Jr., NOAA

A Hamoa resident, Henry Kahula, also had a harrowing story to tell interviewers after the tsunami: "Boy, you don't see nothing but dirty water going out. And when I went around there you see all kind of type of fish on the ground. You see eels, and what you call this kind of octopus. All this darn thing all scattered around. Boy, you had lot of people coming later run to grab the fish."

A Hamoa home after the 1946 Tsunami.
Courtesy Hana Cultural Center

The 1946 Tsunami flattened this Hamoa home.
Courtesy Hana Cultural Center

(Above) Paia, Maui, during the 1946 Tsunami. This photo shows a secondary wave approaching the beach area and the extent of the inundation produced by the first wave. National Oceanographic and Atmospheric Administration

(Left) This photograph was taken on the Big Island showing the power of the 1946 tsunami. National Oceanographic and Atmospheric Administration

The 1946 Tsunami devastated this Hilo store.
National Oceanographic and Atmospheric Administration

After the 1946 Tsunami, the cleanup took years. Location unknown.
National Oceanographic and Atmospheric Administration

Before the Hana Highway, cars and horses were the only way to get from Kailua to Ke'anae.

3 The Hana Highway

Hana Highway nowadays is more of an endurance drive than a scenic drive; there are more than fifty bridges and very sharp, (sometimes) blind curves. But the rain forests and views are terrific. Unfortunately, some tourists do not appreciate its importance in Maui's history or how difficult it was to build.

Officially, it was designated as the "Hana Belt Road Historic District" and, in the sixteenth century, Maui chiefs Pi'ilani and Kihapi'ilani built it as the "King's Trail." The original road was only a trail: it was four to six feet wide, 138 miles long, and paved with hand-fitted lava rocks.

During the late 1800s and early 1900s, travelers ventured around Hana on horseback, following the King's Trail and the Ko'olau Ditch. In 1908, reinforced concrete bridges were built along the coast in anticipation of major road upgrades. By 1926, the Hana Belt Road was a key component of the road system around Maui. And until the late 1960s the Hana Highway was not paved. It's still an adventure! A poet tries to understand the highway:

"I see us along Hana's highway—you at the wheel I last wielded alone curving from waterfall to waterfall their long thin threads like spider floss or glycerin spun out by some Hawaiian deity we can feel, not see plunging in virginal straightness into alluring dark pools mist captured in tropical branchings of ginger, plumeria, one-handed at the wheel you're laughing at this ceaselessness of curves and so many misleading one-way signs."

Courtesy Mary Oliver

An early motorist on the road to Hana had it all to himself.

Hana Highway under construction in the 1920s. Courtesy Maui Electric Company.

Two men by an automobile looking at the Ke'anae coast on the road to Hana. This section opened in 1925.
Hawaiian Historical Society

Koukou'ai Bridge between Haiku and Kipahulu, Hana, Maui County, Hawaii. Library of Congress

Na'ili'iliha'ele Bridge between Haiku and Kipahulu. Library of Congress

On the Hana Highway, the Waikani Bridge was one of the most impressive bridges ever built in Hawaii. It was completed in 1926. The Hana Highway is listed on the state and national registers of historic places. It has 59 bridges and eight culverts more than 50 years old. Most are one-lane bridges under state jurisdiction, with the county claiming responsibility for 14 bridges south of Hana town.

In the 1970s, this enterprising roadside artist was looking for a buyer of his Waikani Bridge painting.

Lush vegetation along the Hana Highway.

Road-scape in vicinity of culvert with horseshoe curve on Hana Highway between Haiku and Hana. Library of Congress

The Hana Highway affords motorists spectacular views of the coastline.

Tight and sometimes blind corners are the norm on the Hana Highway.

Ke'anae has plenty of taro patches, few homes, and a church.

Ke'anae Church. Hawaii Tourism Authority/ Tor Johnson

Ke'anae Taro ponds.

Pi'ilanihale Heiau

Off the Hana Highway, the Pi'ilani Heiau, the largest such historic site in Hawaii, dominates the landscape. Its northern wall is fifty feet high with five terraced steps. From space it stands out. The *heiau* is located on a bluff in East Maui, four miles north of Hana, and has been incorporated into the Kahanu Garden, which is part of the National Tropical Botanical Gardens.

The name Pi'ilanihale means "House of Pi'ilani" in the Hawaiian language. The history of this *heiau* is shrouded in mystery. Perhaps Hana chiefs built it when Maui was divided between two ruling chiefs—one in Hana and the other in the rest of Maui. Chief Pi'ilani rededicated it in the sixteenth century when he united all of Maui.

© Google Earth

Just south of Hana, the Hana Highway goes by lush cattle pastures and affords the viewer great views of the Hana coastline.

St. Peter's Church, Puuiki. © Bruce McAllister

A relic in Kipahulu area. © Bruce McAllister

Between Puuiki and Kipahulu watch out for pigs and Green Bay Packer Drive.
Courtesy of DOCUMERICA

The old Morris home in Puuiki. © Bruce McAllister

Paul Fagan (left) and Johnny Hanchett (right). Hanchett managed the original Hotel Hana-Maui and the Hana Ranch.

4. Paul Fagan: Cattle, Hotel & Baseball

After Hana's sugar boom in the 1880s, this isolated town went into a depression in the 1940s, with its population dropping to less than five hundred. In the 1930s, Paul Fagan, an entrepreneur from San Francisco, bought the Hana Sugar Company from the Unna Brothers. In 1944, he decided Hana was a great place to live, saw long-range opportunities in Hana, and replaced the sugar cane fields with high-quality range grass and three hundred imported Hereford cattle. The same year he gave up his cattle ranch on Molokai and bought fourteen thousand acres of land in and around Hana.

Soon Fagan developed a special bond with the locals and even contemplated retiring there. Fagan then started the Ka'uiki Inn in 1946 for his friends; he was also thinking of adding tourism to his investments. This would soon expand into what became known as the Hotel Hana-Maui.

But on April 1, 1946, a huge tsunami struck Hawaii, pounding the Hana coastline and killing a dozen locals. Eventually, Hana recovered and most of its residents soon found jobs at the ranch and hotel.

In 1947, to highlight his new resort, Fagan brought his entire baseball team, the San Francisco Seals, to Hana for spring training. The shrewd businessman knew that major league baseball—strictly an East Coast activity in those days—could not ignore everything west of the Mississippi for much longer, especially in the large cities of California. With that in mind, in 1944, he quietly assumed majority interest of the San Francisco Seals.

Two years later, Fagan put carefully laid plans into motion, which, when completed, would transform the Pacific Coast League into the third major league. Fagan made Lefty O'Doul the highest-paid skipper in all of professional ball, rewarded his players with big league salaries and luxury accommodations, and upgraded Seals Stadium into a prominent ballpark in the United States.

His baseball investment paid off handsomely with a PCL pennant in 1946 and a minor league single-season attendance record of 670,563. His fast track to the big leagues also took on frightening reality to major league owners, who suddenly understood the deep-pocketed Fagan meant business. Celebrating the league crown, Fagan decided to prepare his Seals for the 1947 season at Hana, Maui. Not only would it serve as a combination of spring training and reward for the players, but also a large group of West Coast writers would accompany the team, giving his resort free newspaper exposure.

The San Francisco Seals touched down at Kahului Airport on February 24, 1947, in a Matson DC-4 *Skymaster*, twelve hours and ten minutes after leaving Oakland Airport; it was the first direct commercial passenger flight to a neighboring island. Once they arrived in Hana, the team worked out at an old school field in the shadow of Ka'uiki cinder cone—home of the demigod Maui, and birthplace of Ka'ahumanu, arguably the most powerful woman in the history of Hawaii. This was a very shrewd public relations move because sportswriters accompanying the team saw Hana as a Shangri-La and wrote glowing reviews of this isolated paradise. They dubbed it "Heavenly Hana."

In 1960, Paul Fagan passed away, but his dreams for a prosperous Hana had succeeded. In his honor, a massive cross was erected on Lyon's Hill above the village. A recent census showed Hana's population at over 1,200 people. Tourism and the ranch have kept the village reasonably healthy. Affluent second homeowners, a successful cattle ranch, and the hotel (now known as the Travaasa) have sustained Hana.

The original Hotel Hana-Maui. Hawaii State Archives

Boats often towed cattle to freighters.
Hawaii State Archives

Moving cattle to ship. Date, location unknown.
Hawaii State Archives

An Hawaiian *paniolo* (cowboy). The Hawaiian cowboy culture emerged back in the 1800s and to this day remains insular and completely unique to Hawaii with its own music, rituals, and language. Hawaii State Archives

A full load of cattle. Hawaii State Archives

Hana Ranch cattle have plenty of rich grass. Courtesy of DOCUMERICA

Hana cattle can be tough to handle. © Bruce McAllister

Cattle drive near downtown Hana.
© Bruce McAllister

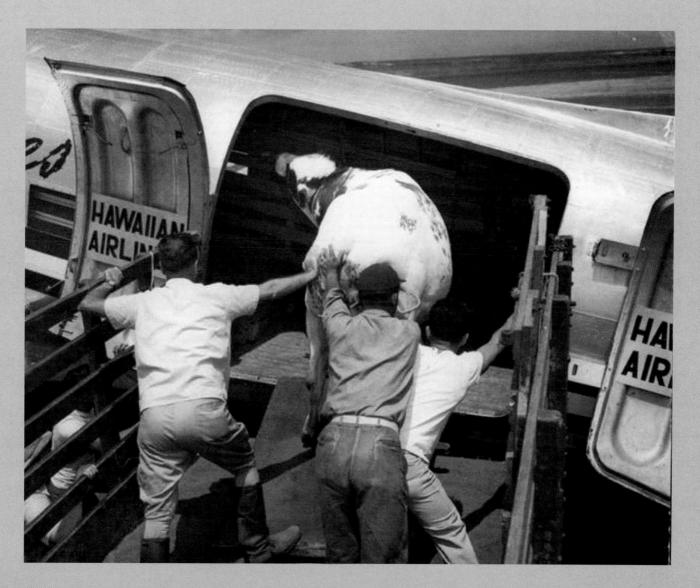

Even Hawaiian Airlines DC-3 aircraft were used to haul cattle in the old days. And once in a while a pig or two might be aboard en route to a luau. Hawaii State Archives

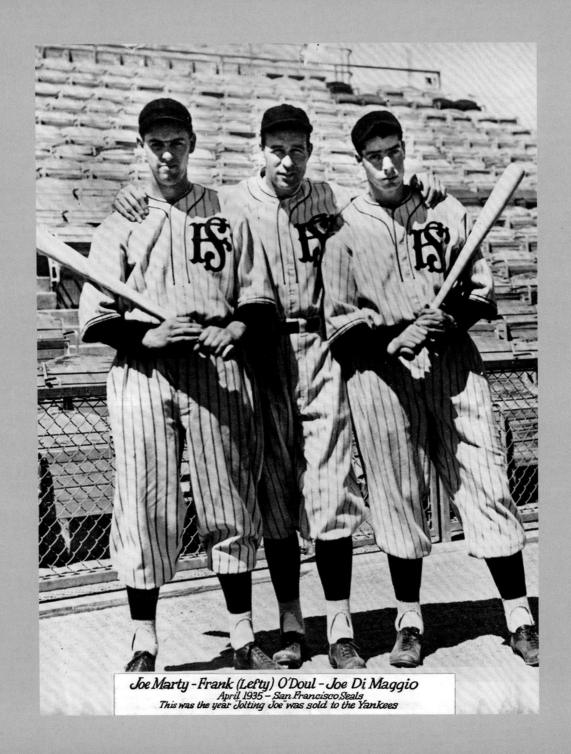

Joe Marty - Frank (Lefty) O'Doul - Joe DiMaggio
April 1935 — San Francisco Seals
This was the year "Jolting Joe" was sold to the Yankees

From his stadium office, Paul Fagan watching a San Francisco Seals game.
© Bruce McAllister

In their heyday, the San Francisco Seals dominated the Pacific Coast League.

This Matson DC-4 carried the entire San Francisco Seal team and sportswriters from Oakland to Hawaii. The flight took over twelve hours.

Lea Matsuda (third from the left), Seals player unidentified, and Fontanella (right). Other children unidentified.
San Francisco Public Library

The San Francisco Seals returning to San Francisco aboard the *SS Lurline* after spring training in Hana and a few exhibition games with the New York Giants in Honolulu. San Francisco Public Library

Hana's baseball field. Fagan's Hill is in the background. Courtesy DOCUMERICA

John Helekahi with kids watching a baseball game at Hana's baseball field. © Bruce McAllister

(Left) A long view of Fagan's Hill.
© Bruce McAllister

Fagan's Hill at sunrise.

Harolen Kaiwi of the Hana Cultural Center / Museum. Both photos © Bruce McAllister

Established by *kupuna* (wise elders) to perpetuate the traditional way of life of Hana, the Hana Cultural Center (left) houses ancient artifacts, including a Hawaiian quilt, poi boards, stone implements, fish nets, and hooks. There is also an interesting portrait display with stories about past Hana leaders.

5 Hotel Hana-Maui

In 1946, the last sugar plantation in Hana closed, signaling the end of the sugar industry in Hana. Many families, unable to find work, moved to plantations on the other side of the island. At the same time, Paul Fagan, a retired entrepreneur from San Francisco, started the Ka'uiki Inn, and it became known as the Hotel Hana-Maui, in an attempt to identify and highlight Hana.

Fagan spared nothing; he had Japanese carpenters customize rooms and the reception area with lauhala and native wood trim. The dining area had a beautiful view of the ocean as well as nearby cottages. After Fagan's death, the hotel survived several owners who did not always have the right management teams in place.

Recently, the resort changed ownership and embarked on an improvement program that vaulted it into the top spot in Hawaii in *Condé Nast Traveler*'s annual Readers' Choice Awards. Rooms have no TV, radio, internet, or air-conditioning. The hotel has a back-to-nature feeling that would appeal to affluent travelers who needed a simple retreat far removed from their usual frenzied lives.

"I see it all the time," said Mark Stebbings, Travaasa managing director. "People are totally drained when they arrive. They can hardly muster a friendly word, but within a couple of days, they're out enjoying life again. They need a place to recharge. This is it."

Despite its remote location, the sixty five-room hotel offers all the trappings of a large resort: fine dining, lounge, spa, tennis courts, infinity pool, yoga, and cultural activities, including throw-net fishing, lei-making, and outrigger lessons in Hana Bay.

The old Hotel Hana-Maui lobby.
Hawaii State Archives

Hana-Maui personnel in the 1950s: Kahuila (left), Fanny Kahuila (second from the left), MonaLisa Kalalau (third from the left), and Sophie Kaiwi (right). © Bruce McAllister

Reception area at the Hotel Hana-Maui in the 1950s.
Hawaii State Archives

The Old Plantation House is currently being used for weddings and special events.
© Travaasa Experiential Resorts

Johnny Pi'ilani Watkins was a gifted performer whose talents included chanter, dancer, teacher, composer, singer, musician, choreographer, and recording artist. In the 1950s, he worked at the Hotel Hana-Maui and was a big draw for guests, doing shows with some of the hotel employees. In 1955, after a stint as an entertainer on O'ahu, Watkins took 48 dancers to New York where they performed on Broadway. He became head musician and choreographer and starred in the Broadway production of Paradise Island with Guy Lombardo and June Taylor.

A Hotel Hana-Maui receptionist in the 1950s.
© Bruce McAllister

The original Hotel Hana-Maui bar had a bush flavor with all kinds of shotguns and stuffed pheasants. On his visit to Hana, Clark Gable held court in this bar. Hawaii State Archives

(Right) In 2010, seven rare oil paintings by Arman Tateos Manookian (1904–1931) were removed from the Hotel Hana-Maui and sold. Helene Fagan, the wife of Hana Ranch Founder Paul Fagan, first purchased the paintings, which depict images of early Hawaiians and the arrival of Captain Cook, from the artist in 1929. Until the Fagans sold Hotel Hana-Maui, they were the only Manookian oil paintings known to be on public display anywhere in the world. In the end, even a group of Hawaiian investors could not keep the priceless paintings in Hawaii.

Paul Fagan spared no expense, using Japanese carpenters to build the Hotel Hana-Maui. Who wouldn't want to have breakfast here? © Travaasa Experiential Resorts

Travaasa's lobby water feature. © Travaasa Experiential Resorts

The Travaasa's Sea Cottages. © Travaasa Experiential Resorts

© Travaasa Experiential Resorts

(Left) Sea Cottages in the evening. © Travaasa Experiential Resorts

Yoga at sunrise. © Travaasa Experiential Resorts

(right) Hotel guests have always enjoyed horse rides along the spectacular Hana coastline. Paul Fagan brought the original hotel horses all the way from California. © Bruce McAllister

Larry Kaikala at Seven Sacred Pools (Oʻheʻo Gulch) before it became part of Haleakala National Park.

6 Faces of Hana

The lure of this isolated yet beautiful town is enough to make one think twice before moving to the outside world. The faces of the natives say it all: smiles. Maybe it's the trade winds or the rain forests but, whatever it is, there is an inner happiness in those who live in the Hana district. Most likely, it's because Hana never changes; it protects its identity and the outside world cannot change its character.

Peter Pi'ilani at Hamoa Beach in 1949.
All photos in Chapter Six © Bruce McAllister

Andrew Park at Hamoa Beach in the 1950s. Later he turned Hana's dump into a first-class recycling center that looked more like a garden than an eyesore.

Andrew Park in 2017.

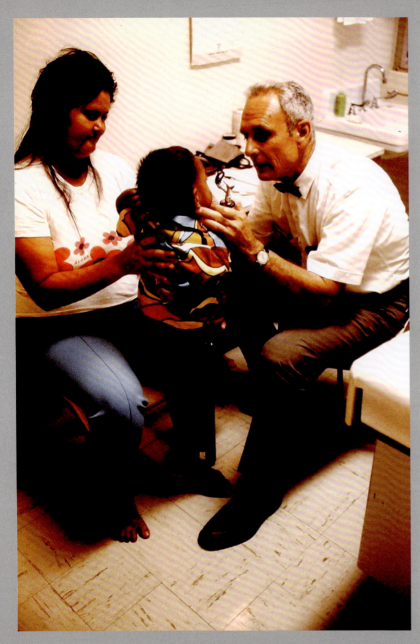 

Dr. Milton Howell was Hana's doctor for decades and beloved by Hana residents. He also took care of Charles Lindbergh during the famous aviator's last days.

Tiny Malaikini with babies at a Hana Bay party.

A party at Hana Bay.

Solomon Hoopai working on fishing nets and closeup opposite page. © Bruce McAllister

Annamae Redo picking papayas.

Wilfred Kala worked as a lifeguard at Hamoa Beach and then at the Hana Ranch.

Chester Pua, coconut tree trimmer.
Courtesy Dot Pua.

Fish feast at Hana Bay.

Old-timer plays an imaginary ukulele outside the old Hasegawa Store.
© Bruce McAllister

 Hasegawa General Store

The Hasegawa family has operated a general store in Hana since 1910. Four generations of Hasegawas have kept the store going, making it the longest surviving shop in Hana. Since Hasegawa's great-grandfather, Shoichi, and great-granduncle, Saburo, opened the store in 1910, Hana has changed little. If anything, the sleepy village made famous in Paul Weston's 1961 song has shrunk from a once bustling plantation town with several stores, inns, and a population of more than three thousand, to what it is today.

When the sugar plantation shut down at the end of the Second World War, most Japanese families left Hana but the Hasegawa's survived. Later a fire destroyed the original store, but the Hasegawas found a replacement nearby: the old movie theater.

Neil Hasegawa now runs the store and relates its importance to the community. "Here in Hana, when you have a business, you've got a lot of responsibility with the community too. The decisions we make affect everybody," Hasegawa said. "It's not just as cut and dry as it would be on O'ahu. There are a lot of things that come into play."

Today's Hasegawa General Store has become a focal point for both locals and tourists. Need a critical plumbing part? Hasegawa's has it. The narrow aisles inside the tin-roof store are jam packed with a little bit of everything from food to sunscreen.

Hasegawa's was immortalized by Paul Weston's 1961 hit, "The Hasegawa General Store" ("You'll find a baseball bat and a piano hat, sunburn creams and the latest magazines, muumuu's, mangoes and ukuleles..."), which premiered on the old "Hawaii Calls" radio show and over the years has been recorded by everyone from Arthur Godfrey to Hilo Hattie to part-time Hana residents Jim Nabors and Carol Burnett.

Wandering the aisles, you'll find locally made vodka (distilled from pineapples) on a shelf near the plumbing supplies and motor oil. Papaya butter is across the aisle from the fishing gear, and rubber boots line a shelf above the locally grown tomatoes. And there is surfboard wax, video rentals, dog food, watches, machetes, aloha dolls, ice cream, and SPAM musabi (called "SPAM sushi" by mainlanders). And if you can't find it, Hasegawa General Store will special order it for you.

Harry Hasegawa (left) with Arthur Godfrey (center) at the original Hasegawa General Store in the 1950s.

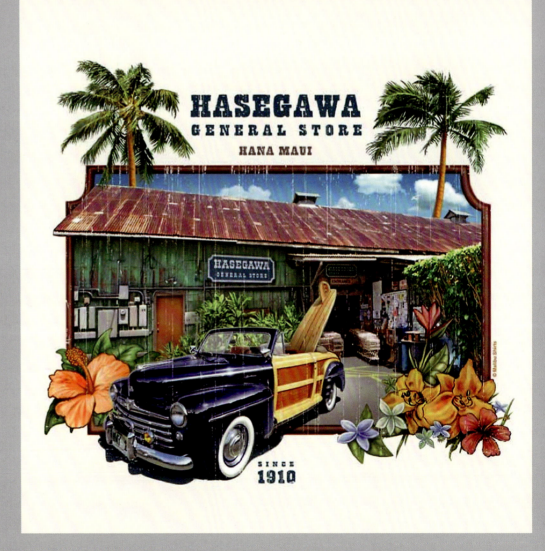

(Left) Hilo Hattie immortalized Paul Weston's Hasegawa poem. Hasegawa General Store even had its own men's aloha shirts. © Malibu Shirts.

On the island of Maui
Far from Waikiki
There's a place called Hana
That is heavenly

And when you go there
You've got to see
The Hasegawa General Store

As you walk through the doorway
What a great surprise
There's a wonderful
Variety of merchandise

It's all spread out there
Before your eyes
At the Hasegawa General Store

They've got a baseball hat
A paniolo hat
Sunburn creams
And the latest magazines
Muu muus, mangos and ukuleles too
And even hamburger for a malahini like you

They say a cheerful 'aloha' when you first go by
And a sweet 'mahalo nui' when you say 'bye-bye'
You can't resist it, once you try
The Hasegawa General Store

You've gotta walk very slowly
As your tour begins

Through those pineapples, cereals, and bobby pins
Spears and goggles and swimming fins
At the Hasegawa General Store

Now if you want to lama lama
They've got kerosene
If you want to lomi lomi
They've got rubbing cream
Some guava jelly that's just supreme
At the Hasegawa General Store

They've got kukui nuts
Assorted cold cuts
Surfer's pants
And papaya plants
A shiny koa calabash
To catch your eye
Some okolehao
When your throat gets dry

So if you're ever in Hana
With some time to spare
You've got to holo holo
Down to you-know-where

You just name it
They've got it there
At the Hasegawa General Store

© Paul Weston 1963

Stella Perry (left) chatting outside Hasegawa General Store.

Neil Hasegawa now runs Hasegawa General Store. The store was a movie theater in the old days and Paul Fagan installed a dedicated cry baby booth so that everybody could enjoy weekly movies. © Bruce McAllister

Eddie Pu and friends after a day at Hamoa Beach.
© Bruce McAllister

8 Eddie Pu (1929-2012)

WHEREAS, Eddie Pu is a humble and compassionate individual, an outstanding Hawaiian elder whose reputation as a spiritual and cultural leader is widely known on the island of Maui; and

WHEREAS, Eddie Pu knows the importance of the aina, the land, where he has spent every working day of his life, first as a lifeguard at a beach in Hana, Maui, then as one of the first park rangers of O'he'o Gulch, a series of pools and falls that now form a part of Haleakala National Park; and

WHEREAS, Eddie Pu has shared a deep love of the land with thousands of residents and visitors and has even saved many lives, including those of the Saudi ambassador and his wife and son, who experienced trouble at O'he'o Gulch and were swept out to sea; and

WHEREAS, Eddie Pu reconnects to the life and energy of the land and his native Hawaiian ancestors by annually walking the one-hundred-fifty-mile Pi'ilani trail, an ancient trail that encircled the island of Maui and connected villages and heiau scattered on Maui's coastal areas; and

WHEREAS, Eddie Pu's spiritual trek, which takes him several weeks to complete, has raised awareness of the Pi'ilani Trail's native and endemic plants, archaeological sites, artifacts, and burial sites that need to be preserved for the public and future generations; and

WHEREAS, through his words, actions, and lifestyle, Eddie Pu serves as an excellent role model for the people of Hawaii; now, therefore,

BE IT RESOLVED by the House of Representative of the Twenty-fourth Legislature of the State of Hawaii, that this body hereby recognizes and honors Eddie Pu for his contributions, efforts, and achievements in perpetuating native Hawaiian culture and traditions and wishes him continued success in all his future endeavors." (2007)

Eddie Pu was my lifelong friend, and I always admired his upbeat, outgoing nature. As a teenager I spent days with him at Hamoa Beach. Just years before his health problems slowed him down, he would be out on the Hana Highway as a traffic guard when Hana School let out. He used to take walks with Charles Lindbergh. And most important of all, he connected with everyone.

Eddie Pu getting a haircut at the Morris house in Puuiki. © Bruce McAllister

Eddie Pu at Hamoa went spearfishing and played the ukulele when he didn't have to look out for swimmers in distress.
© Bruce McAllister

137

(left) Eddie about to go spear fishing and (right) keeping an eye on swimmers. © Bruce McAllister

On his numerous solo trips around the entire island of Maui, Eddie followed the Kings Highway. It was built with rounded rocks laid into lava beds. He carried a staff to protect himself from unfriendly dogs. Locals gave him food and water when necessary.
(left photo) Library of Congress

For saving the lives of the Saudi ambassador and his family at Seven Pools, Eddie Pu went to Washington, D.C., to accept an award for his bravery from the secretary of the interior. At the time, Eddie was a national park ranger. Man on the left unidentified. Courtesy Vance Pu

Hamoa Beach. © Travaasa Experiential Resorts

9 Beaches

Wai'anapanapa State Park Beach has plenty of parking and full amenities, and it is a popular tourist stop for good reason. It is Maui's only pure black sand beach and its character is truly unique. Lava rock spires jut out into crystal-clear waters, and there is a blowhole that gets active during high surf. During milder wave activity one can easily visit the lava tube at the closer end of the beach by finding the user-friendly stairs.

Hana Bay is ideal for picnics and on summer days, and you might notice the outrigger canoe club practicing. It's a beautiful large black sand beach in a protected cove and is large and crescent shaped, running parallel to the frontage road that leads to the pier. Hana Bay is typically calm and is a great place for swimming, canoeing, and kayaking. There are picnic benches along a grassy area just off the beach that is a popular place for picnics.

Kaihalulu Bay (Red Sands Beach) is not for swimming and has dangerous access. Locals do not use it either.

Koki Beach is a short drive from the town of Hana and is centered among several Hawaiian heritage sites. It's a beautiful crescent of soft sand curves along the bottom of a striking red-and-yellow-striped cinder cliff with great views. The ocean conditions fluctuate here, and currents can be tricky. Usually, water is safest in the summer. It's best to see if locals are in the water; they know when it's safe to swim.

Hamoa Beach is a must-see for any Hana visit. It is only two and a half miles from town, and you will be surprised when you first see this spectacular beach. Author James Michener once stated that this was the most beautiful beach in the world. There are several pavilions behind that beach that are part of the Travaasa Hotel and are exclusively for the usage of their guests. However, by law, all Hawaii beaches are public and open to all. Ocean conditions fluctuate here from calm to fierce, so it's wise to be careful while swimming here when the surf is up.

A Hamoa bather. © Travaasa Experiential Resorts

Hotel guests get beach chairs, umbrellas, and boogy boards at Hamoa Beach.

(above) Looking north from Koki Beach. Courtesy of Danielle Hattori. (right) Signs warn newcomers about strong currents and undertow. © Bruce McAllister

Hana Bay. © Bruce McAllister

Hana Bay. Hawaii Tourism Authority/ Tor Johnson

In 2014, an outrigger race from Keokea (Big Island) enters Hana Harbor, before proceeding from Hana to Kahului. © Gloria Reed / HSCA

Red Sands Beach near Hana is not for tourists or locals. Access is extremely dangerous.

(Left) Venus Pools south of Hana. Tourists' vehicles often clog the Hana Highway near Venus Pools, so it's better to bike or hike there.
© Travaasa Experiential Resorts

Wai'anapanapa Beach.
© Bruce McAllister

(Right) Wai'anapanapa Beach has ample parking, picnic tables, and distinctive black sand. Some tourists explore nearby lava tubes.
© Travaasa Experiential Resorts

An Inter-Island Sikorsky flight over Haleakala in 1935. Hawaii State Archives

10 Hana by Air

The original Hana Airport was a small grass field located at Hamoa. Inter-Island Airways served the Hana area with eight-passenger Sikorsky amphibians from May 1935 to the beginning of World War II. At that point, newer sixteen-passenger amphibians and twenty-four-passenger land planes served the islands but were too big for the short Hamoa field. Scheduled service was discontinued and the entire Hana area fell victim to technological development and became dependent on the infrequent service of charter aircraft. Most of the charter flights to Hana in those days originated out of Honolulu and were flown by ex-Navy pilots. As a teenager in the 1950s, I was on some of those flights, and it was exciting to take off from the Hamoa airstrip; we would just clear the Koki Beach surf as we lifted off. It was quite exciting!

Although Hana is approximately fifty-five miles from Kahului by road, it's a challenging drive of two and a half hours to three hours. It was time for a change. The increase in population and the growth of Hotel Hana-Maui justified scheduled airline operations into the Hana area.

A new airport was constructed and opened to scheduled traffic on November 11, 1950. The land was owned in part by the territory, and the balance donated by Hana Ranch Company. The federal government, through the Civil Aviation Authority (CAA), participated in the cost of developing the facilities.

In 1955, the airport consisted of 125 acres of land, and had one paved runway, 8-26, which was one hundred feet wide and 3,600 feet long. Hawaiian Airlines was Hana's only scheduled service to Kahului or Honolulu. The new airport had a passenger terminal building, a freight terminal building, taxiways, paved plane parking area, wind socks, field maintenance, crash-fire protection, and ground transportation services.

As late as 1975, Hana Airport had no control tower and just the one paved, lighted runway. It had one crash-fire vehicle and a single attendant. Only nonscheduled small aircraft were servicing Hana. At first, water had to be trucked to the new Hana Airport, but eventually water lines were authorized and built.

In the 1930s, a Pan American Airlines crewman helps unload bundled newspapers from an Inter-Island Airways Sikorsky S-38 into an outrigger canoe. Location unknown. Hawaii State Archives

Two years later a project for taxiway and runway resurfacing at Hana was delayed because of load limitations placed on the Hana Highway bridges, over which asphaltic concrete had to be hauled.

The Federal Aviation Administration (FAA) has kept the airport up to date with additional clearing, grading of runway areas, and new fencing to keep out people and cattle. Over the years, scheduled air service to Hana has become more dependable, and regular air service has enhanced Hana's link to the outside world.

An Inter-Island Sikorsky S-43 flies past Molokai. Date unknown. Hawaii State Archives

Inter-Island Sikorsky amphibians were the first commercial aircraft to provide service between the various Hawaiian Islands. Hawaii State Archives

Hana Airstrip near Hamoa, January 9, 1936. Note the eight aircraft on the ground.
Hawaii State Archives

A charter aircraft picking up passengers at the Hamoa Airstrip in the 1940s. Hawaii State Archives

(Left) Clearing land for the Hana Airport. Hawaii State Archives

The Hana Airport has clean approaches and a forgiving 100-feet wide and 3,600-feet long runway.

Often Hana residents have turned out for inaugural flights to and from Hana Airport.

Over the years, different air carriers have operated flights to and from Hana.

The Hana Airport Terminal.

Charles Lindbergh championed many environmental projects during his final years when he wasn't in Kipahulu.

11 Kipahulu and Lindbergh

The Kipahulu lowlands were once heavily populated and offered fertile soil and abundant water, as well as coastal access—all within a relatively small area. Based on stories by early explorers and visitors, as well as archaeological evidence, Kipahulu was a well-populated and intensively cultivated land. Here, archaeologists have discovered the stuff of everyday life—house foundations, taro fields, animal pens, and family shrines. Amongst these ruins are often similar-looking stone structures built during the time of European contact and early settlement of the Hawaiian Islands (1778 to 1850), a time of significant change to traditional Hawaiian culture.

In modern times, Charles Lindbergh, Samuel Pryor Jr., a Pan Am executive, and Lowell Thomas, a former lieutenant governor of Alaska, settled in this remote area. Pryor and Lindbergh had no use for bringing electricity and TV to Kipahulu; they enjoyed a primitive lifestyle along with their privacy. They were strong proponents of re-designating the nearby O'he'o Gulch (Seven Sacred Pools) area as part of Haleakala National Park.

In October 1972, Charles Lindbergh was diagnosed with lymphoma—cancer of the lymph system. The lymphoma soon spread. He tried to beat it, but by the spring of 1974, he had been admitted to Columbia-Presbyterian Hospital in New York City. It became increasingly plain that lymphoma was the one battle that Charles Lindbergh would lose.

Lindbergh looked relaxed before his historic flight across the Atlantic. But he didn't get much sleep the night before his epic flight.

In control as always, Lindbergh checked himself out of Columbia-Presbyterian, against his doctors' advice, to make his last flight. On a stretcher laid across a row of first-class seats, he traveled by United Airlines to his remote home in Hawaii in August of 1974. "I would rather spend one day on Maui than thirty days in the hospital," he said. (It wasn't planned, but one of the pilots of the United DC-8 flight was said to have flown the Spirit of Saint Louis replica as a movie pilot for the Jimmy Stewart film.)

Charles Augustus Lindbergh was buried in a Congregational graveyard at Kipahulu, Hawaii, on August 26, 1974. Lindbergh had specified how his grave was to be dug and lined ("Father was obsessed about drainage," his son Jon later noted), he scripted his funeral and memorial service, and he stipulated the simple materials and design of his "green" eucalyptus wood coffin. The local craftsman, on short notice, had his hands full to complete the large coffin. To this day, the myth endures that Lindbergh was buried standing up, facing the ocean, like an ancient Hawaiian warrior—yet another Lindbergh legend.

Charles Lindbergh and Samuel Pryor Jr. were both buried in the same graveyard in Kipahulu that they had cleared by hand many years before they passed away. Pryor's Gibbon apes were buried near his grave.

After his epic flight across the Atlantic, Lindbergh received a hero's welcome on June 13, 1927, in New York City. He rode up lower Broadway in an open car next to Mayor James J. Walker. Library of Congress

Huge crowds greeted the Spirit of St. Louis when it arrived in Croydon, England.

Toward the end of World War II, Lindbergh served as a technical advisor to the Marines in the South Pacific.

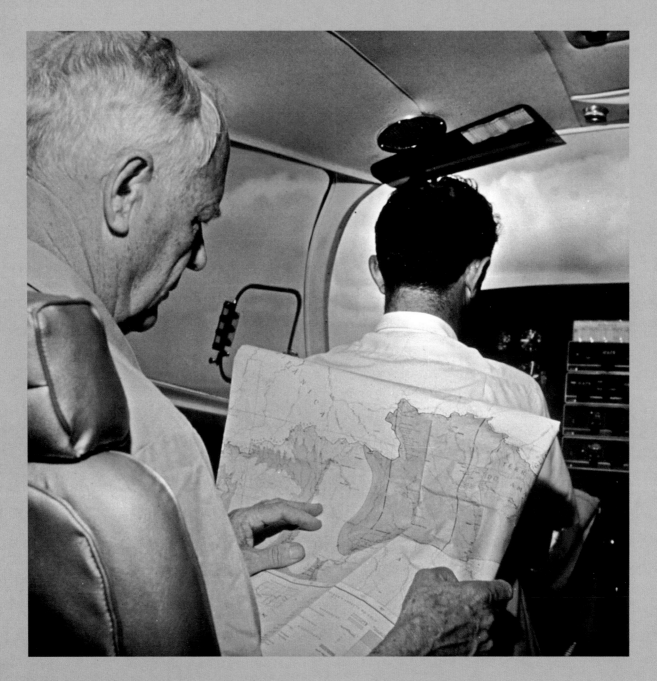
Lindbergh en route to an environmental project.

(left) Kipahulu resident Samuel F. Pryor Jr. with one of his Gibbon apes in 1971. Pryor was an ex-Pan American Airlines executive and he talked Lindbergh into buying land in Kipahulu. Often his apes would accompany him on airline flights until passengers complained and the airlines put an end to apes in the cabin. Whenever Pryor took his apes to the bar at the Hotel Hana-Maui, they would terrify the patrons. His beloved apes are buried with him at the Palapala Ho'omau Church.

Lowell Thomas Jr. in 2003 with his Helio Courier at Anchorage, Alaska. He and Lindbergh were neighbors in Kipahulu and avid environmentalists.
© Bruce McAllister

In their later years, the Lindberghs spent more time in Kipahulu. Charles enjoyed the remoteness of their home there, but Anne did not.

Lindbergh's Hawaii physician, Dr. Milton Howell (left), Sam Pryor Jr. (center), and Lindbergh share a light moment at Kipahulu, Hawaii, in 1971. Lindbergh Picture Collection (MS 325B). Manuscripts and Archives, Yale University Library

The Lindbergh's A-Frame home at Kipahulu, Maui. Anne did not enjoy the primitive lifestyle that her husband embraced. He was against paving the roads near his home and did not want electricity.

Lindbergh and Sam Pryor Jr. restored the Palapala Ho'omau Church and its grounds before both of them passed away.
© Bruce McAllister

In Kipahulu, Maui, Lindbergh directed the construction of his grave before his death. Lava rock lined the ample grave, and the casket was built with local eucalyptus hardwood. There were rumors that the grave was deep enough for Lindbergh to be buried upright like a warrior looking out to sea.

The Hana Post Office honored Charles Lindbergh with this postal cachet ten years after his death.

Lindbergh's grave. © Bruce McAllister

The ocean view from the graveyard where Charles Lindbergh is buried.

With the right conditions, O'he'o Gulch (Seven Sacred Pools) can be safe for swimming. But swimming offshore can be dangerous because of strong undertow and currents.

O'he'o Gulch (Seven Sacred Pools) attracts many tourists and some go swimming when the conditions are safe. © Bruce McAllister

Bamboo forests line the trail near O'he'o Gulch (Seven Sacred Pools) in Haleakala National Park.

The bamboo forest trail near Oʻheʻo Gulch.

In the Kipahulu area, ONO Farms grows several organic fruits and coffee.

12 *Kaupo*

Kaupo is rich in ancient history as told by Hawaiian mythology and archaeological evidence. It is believed that the first Polynesians to arrive in Maui landed on this part of the island.

In ancient times it was said to be the most populated area of Maui as described by Captain La Perouse. This French captain was the first to land on Maui in 1789 and, sailing around from the lush Hana side, he was greeted by hundreds of canoes at Kaupo. The canoes that came alongside his two ships were loaded with trade goods of hogs, bananas, taro, and water for trading with the French frigate. This led Captain La Perouse to surmise that they were not the first Europeans to encounter the Hawaiians. The maps used by Captain Cook, some to explore the South Pacific, were of Spanish origin.

Kaupo was a *Wahipana* (legendary place) for ancient Hawaiians. In the early 1900s many families lived in Kaupo. Fishing, farming, hunting, and ranching were primary occupations. Nowadays taro ponds, ranching, the Kaupo Church, the local store, and the winding Pi'ilani Highway are the only places where tourists stop for a photo op.

(Left) The Kaupo Huialoha Congregational Church.

Mules browsing near the Huialoha Congregational Church at Kaupo. Barren and dry are what you'll see as you approach Kaupo. The tropical vegetation disappears and grasslands are overtaken by volcanic rock instead of vegetation. © Bruce McAllister

Since 1859, the Huialoha Congregational Church at Kaupo has stood sentry on this wind-whipped coastline. © Bruce McAllister

The Kaupo Gap. A popular 8.3 mile route takes hikers "out of the Gap" from the Paliku Cabin within Haleakala National Park. The trail runs downhill through lava formations and various patches of vegetation and dry brush that include native forests and clusters of Kiawe wood. Midway through the hike, the trail departs from the Park boundary and into property owned by the Kaupo Ranch.

Cattle also use the Pi'ilani Highway.

In 1925, Nick Soon started Kaupo Store and it has survived to this day. The store has antique cameras and other knick-knacks. And, for those who have survived all the blind corners on the Pi'ilani Highway, it has soft drinks.

Central to this place is Kaupo School, which is steeped in history. Since its establishment in 1887, the school has served as the only government institution in a remote, isolated landscape. The two-room classroom building and associated Teacher's Cottage were built in 1922–1923. Keiki learned Hawaiian first here, along with other skills such as fishing, hunting, and horseback riding. The school is significant to this remote community as both a gathering place and a link to the ranching and agricultural culture of Kaupo.
Courtesy Historic Hawaii Foundation

Along the Kaupo coast.

One-lane blind corners are the norm along the Pi'ilani Highway.

The Loaloa Heiau is located in Kaupo. This is one of the few remaining intact examples of a large *luakini heiau* (state level temple where human sacrifice was performed). Pihana, also called Pihanakilani and Pi'ihana, was a *luakini* where human sacrifice was carried out. According to accounts written by outsiders, victims were most often kapu breakers or war captives. Once the center of an important cultural complex around Kaupo, oral tradition attributes the construction of the temple at about 1730 AD to Kekaulike, King of Maui, who lived at Kaupo and died in 1736.

Early Hawaiian shrines were simple and constructed by families and small communities. With population growth and changes in religion, social organizations became more complex and large heiau were constructed for public ceremonies. In general, the *ali'i* (chiefs) worshiped four major gods in these ceremonies: Lono (peace, agriculture, fertility), Kane (the creator and ancestral deities), Kanaloa (the ocean, healing and general well-being), and Ku (war).

Ancient Hawaiians had many types of *heiau*, each with their own distinct function and use by particular segments of society. *Heiau* ranged in size from a single upright stone to massive and complex structures. Larger heiau were built by *ali'i*, but the largest and most complex, the *luakini heiau*, could only be constructed and dedicated by an *ali'i 'ai moku* (paramount chief of an independent chiefdom or island). *Luakini heiau* were reserved for rituals involving human or animal sacrifice and highlighted the *ali'i 'ai moku*'s spiritual, economic, political, and social control over his lands and his authority over the life and death of his people. This historic site is not accessible to the public and it is on private property.

© Google Earth

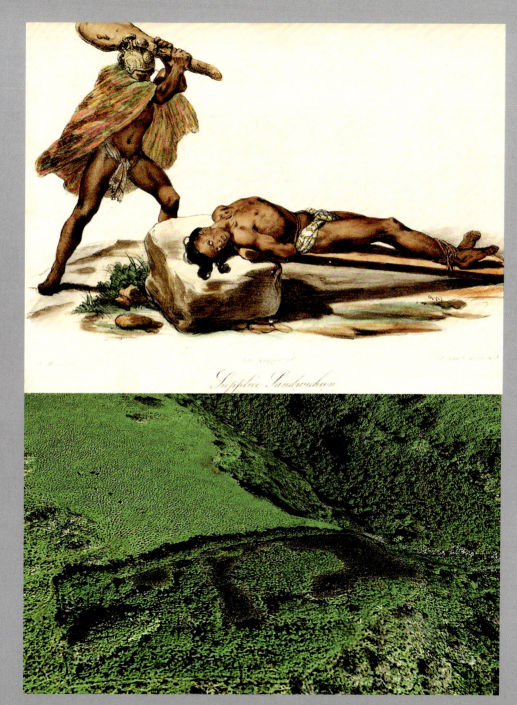

In the Kaupo area, mean annual rainfall is about 50 inches and mean annual temperature is about 75 degrees F. In Hana, by contrast, the mean annual rainfall is about 100 inches. This area is ideal for ranching.

Along the Kaupo coast, cyclists navigate the wiggly Pi'ilani Highway.

13 *Haleakala*

Haleakala is a massive inactive volcano (sometimes named a crater) that forms more than 75 percent of Maui. The surrounding walls are steep and the interior mostly barren-looking, with a scattering of volcanic but colorful cones.

Early Hawaiians applied the name *House of the Sun* to the mountain. Haleakala is also the name of a peak on the southwestern edge of Kaupo Gap. In Hawaiian legend, the depression at the summit of Haleakala was home to the grandmother of the demigod Maui. According to the legend, Maui's grandmother helped him capture the sun and force it to slow its journey in order to lengthen the day.

A United Nations International Biosphere Reserve, the park comprises starkly contrasting worlds of mountain and coast. The road to the summit goes from near sea level to 10,023 feet in just thirty-eight miles. In the 1960s, Charles Lindbergh, Sam Pryor Jr., and Dr. Milton Howell were instrumental in incorporating O'he'o Gulch (Seven Sacred Pools) and part of Kipahulu into Haleakala National Park.

The rare Silversword plant grows only inside Haleakala's crater. National Park Service

Sliding Sands Trail in Haleakala National Park is a eleven-mile trail that features beautiful wild flowers and is only recommended for experienced adventurers. Library of Congress.

In 1909, rangers work on Kalahaku shelter in Haleakala National Park. National Park Service

After a 1936 snowstorm near Haleakala's summit. National Park Service

The original summit house on Haleakala.

Packing in supplies to cabins in Haleakala National Park. National Park Service

By horseback, tourists can see much of the Haleakala Crater.

Reservations are a must for using the few cabins inside Haleakala National Park. National Park Service

Apollo 15 commander Dave Scott and lunar module pilot Jim Irwin scoop up soil inside Haleakala Crater to prepare for their trip to the moon. National Aeronautic and Space Administration

Hikers inside Haleakala Crater.
© Bruce McAllister

The observatories at Haleakala's summit. Haleakala Observatory is one of the most important observing sites in the world. Lying above the tropical inversion layer it experiences superb seeing conditions and dominant clear skies. © Google Earth

Nene birds inside Haleakala National Park. The Nene bird is the state bird of Hawaii. By 1950, there were fewer than 50 of them in the wild. Hawaiian Park Rangers strive to bring them back. National Park Service

Shortly before his death, Clark Gable visited Hana on vacation. At the time he was getting ready for his role in the *Misfits*, which also starred Marilyn Monroe. © United Artists

14 Hana's Celebrities

The number of Hollywood celebrities who have visited and/or built a second home in the Hana area is mind-boggling. Charles Lindbergh's life in Hana is described in another chapter. But perhaps one of the most interesting visitors ever was the King of Hollywood, Clark Gable. In 1957, before he did his last movie, Gable took a break at the then Hotel Hana-Maui. He could hardly get a drink at the bar! Local women seemed to come out of the walls. Hana locals normally leave celebrities alone and protect their privacy. Some celebrities came to Hana to "hide out" from everyday paparazzi.

But some actually come to become part of the community, like Kris Kristofferson and Jim Nabors. Kristofferson and his family have lived in Hana since 1990, and he still does concerts benefiting various charities, including the Hana High School, its athletic program, and O'hana Makamae, which provides critical family services in Hana. Jim Nabors developed a 500-acre macadamia nut and flower farm north of Hana that he owned for twenty-five years before selling it to the National Tropical Botanical Gardens, a preservationist organization.

(Top left) Vincent Price

James Michener (top right) proclaimed Hamoa beach the finest beach in the world. Fifteen minutes down the coast from Hana, it is, said Michener, "so perfectly formed that I wonder at its comparative obscurity. The only beach I've ever seen that looks like South Pacific was in the North Pacific."

(Right) Jim Nabors

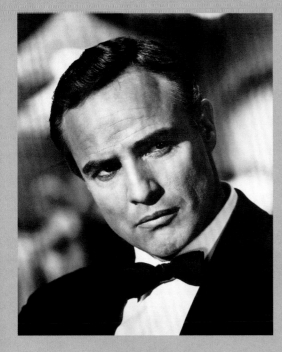

(Top left) Marlon Brando

(Top right) Richard Pryor

(Bottom left and right) Arthur Godfrey

(Left) Carol Burnett

(Right) Oprah Winfrey

(Bottom left) Kris Kristofferson

(Bottom right) George Harrison

(Top right) Woody Harrelson

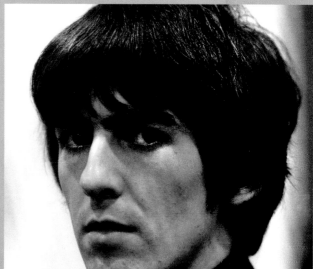

Bibliography

Ariyoshi, Rita, *MAUI On My Mind* Mutual Publishing of Honolulu, 1985

Crowe, Ellie &William, *Exploring Hawaii*, Island Heritage Publishing, Waipahu, 2008

Davis, Lynn Ann & Foster, Nelson, *A Photographer in the Kingdom: Christian J. Hedemann's Early Images of Hawai'i*, Bernice Pauahi Bishop Museum Special Publication, Honolulu, 1989

Ibid, *Na Pa'i Ki'i: The Photographers in the Hawaiian Islands, 1845–1900*, Bishop Museum Special Publication 69, Honolulu, 1980

Engledow, Jill, *Haleakala: A History of the Mountain*, Maui Island Press, Wailuku, HI, 2012

Fernander, Abraham, *Selections from Hawaiian Antiquities & Folklore*, University Press, Honolulu, 1982

Goldman, Rita, *Every Grain of Rice: Portraits of Maui's Japanese Community*, Donning Co., Virginia Beach, VA, 2003

Harden, M. J., *Voices of Wisdom: Hawaiian Elders Speak*, Aka Press, Kula, 1999

Kepler, Angela Kay, *Maui's Hana Highway*, Mutual Publishing, Honolulu, 1987

Kirch, Patrick V., Kuaaina Kahiko: Life and Land in Ancient Kahikinui, Maui, University of Hawaii Press, Honolulu, 2014

Malo, David, *Hawaiian Antiquities*, Bishop Museum Special Publication 2, Honolulu, 1951

McDermott, John F. & Andrade, Naleen N., *People & Culture of Hawaii*, University of Hawaii Press, Honolulu, 2011

McGregor, Davianna Pomaika'i, *Na Kua'aina: Living Hawaiian Culture*, University of Hawaii Press, Honolulu, 2007

Pryor III, Sam, *Make It Happen: The Fascinating Life of Sam Pryor, Jr.*, Self Published, 2008

Seiden, Allan, *The Hawaiian Monarchy*, Mutual Publishing, Honolulu, 2005

Sterling, Elspeth P., *Sights of Maui*, Bishop Museum, Honolulu, 1989

Stevens, Tom, *Islands of Wonder: MAUI*, Mutual Publishing, Honolulu, 2012

Wenkam, Robert, *MAUI: The Last Hawaiian Place*, Friends of The Earth, New York, NY, 1970

Youngblood, Ron, *On the Hana Coast: Being an Accounting of Adventures, Past and Present, in a Land where the Hand of Man Seems to Rest Lightly*, Emphasis Intl., Honolulu, 1983

NEWSPAPER ARTICLES

New York Times Travel Section, *In the Land of the Lotus Eaters*, Patricia Brown, September 30, 2007

Honolulu Advertiser, *Hasegawa General Store Still An Icon*, August 13, 2008

About the Author

Bruce McAllister spent his teenage summers in the 1950s in Puuiki, between Hana and Kipahulu. He was good friends with Eddie Pu and loved to body surf at Hamoa Beach. He wasn't a good surfboarder or spear fisherman. But he photographed Hana life in the late 1940s and 1950s, and many of the photographs in this book were taken with Kodachrome film. His Hana nickname was "Akuhead Pupule" (after a World War II Honolulu radio host).

Since the year 2000, he has authored ten books on aviation history, covering such diverse subjects as Charles Lindbergh, the ageless DC-3, the Arctic, the Alaska Highway, airline stewardesses, and the Berlin Airlift. His books can be previewed at www.wingsalcan.com.